HOW TO DRAW YOUR PET ANIMALS

Jennifer Bell

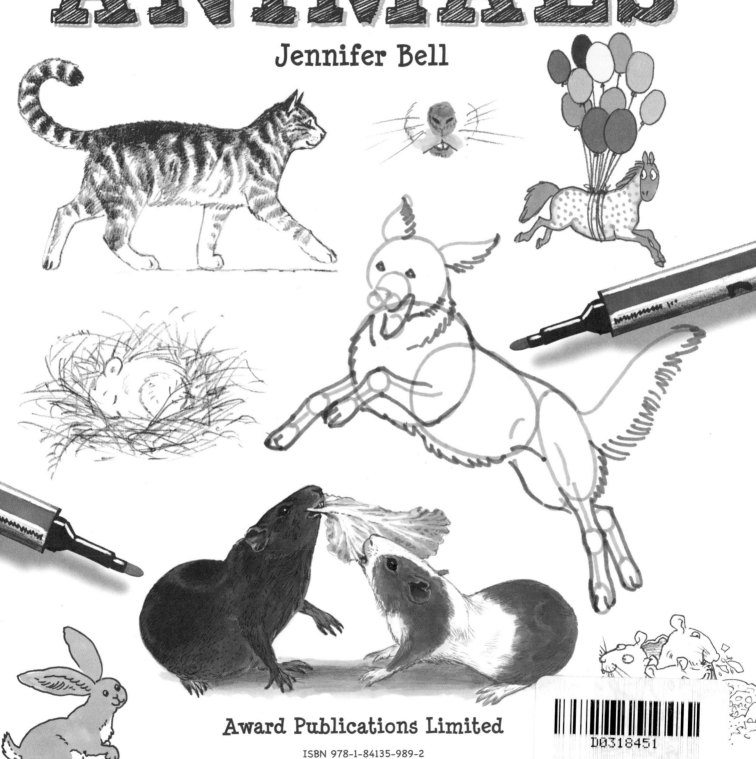

Award Publications Limited

ISBN 978-1-84135-989-2

Published by Award Publications Limited, The Old Riding School, The Welbeck Estate, Worksop, S80 3LR

15 1 Printed in China

D0318451

How to Draw Pets...

...the easy way!

Start SIMPLE

Practise drawing circles...

circles

...and ovals. They don't have to be perfect!

ovals

Draw circles that go behind other circles.

This is the start of turning 2D shapes into 3D pets!

Overlapping shapes become little animals!

Drawing cartoons can help you make realistic drawings.

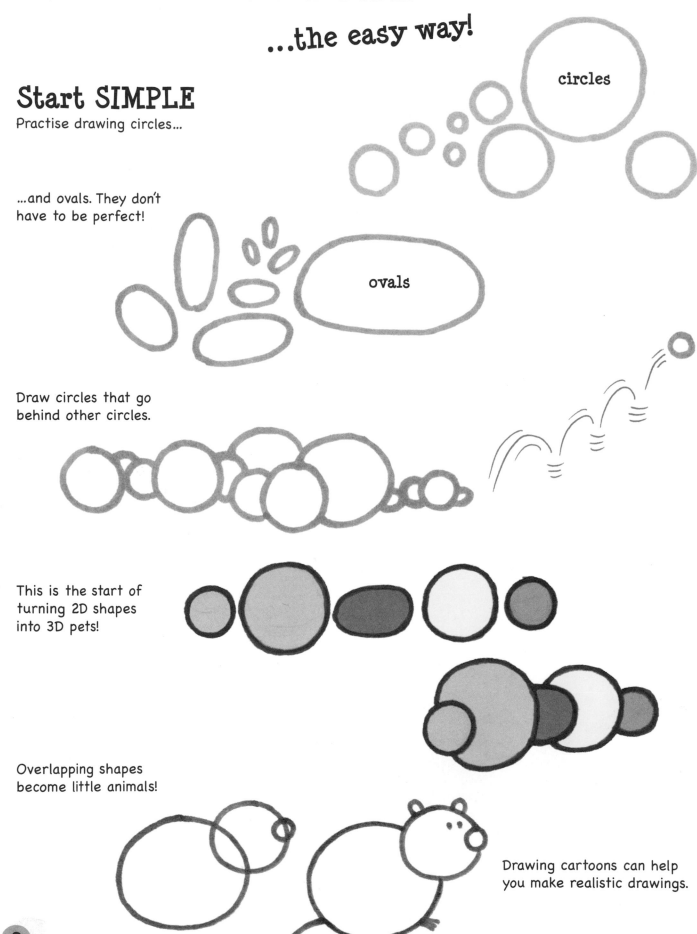

Putting the bits together

Faces and ears

Very simple shapes.

Animal faces often use circles for the front and wedges for the side.

Use good quality pencils and felt pens with thin and thick ends for colouring and blending.

Putting it together – which shapes are the same and which are different?

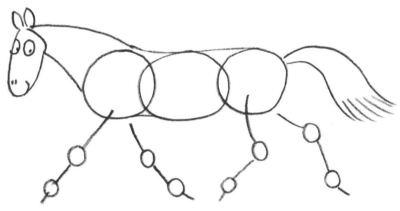

Circles and lines are drawn in different ways for different animals, but most animals start with an oval for a middle then other shapes for shoulders and rumps.

Some animals have long legs; others are very short!

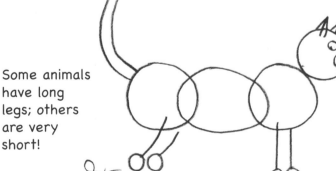

The diagrams in this book are drawn in felt pen. You can copy them in light-coloured felt pen and then go over them in pencil, or use pencil right from the start.

Guinea Pig

Step 1 ▲ Start with a big circle for the shoulders and a large oval for the tummy and back end.

Step 2 ▶ Add ovals for a head and two small ears. Draw two more ovals for the tops of the legs.

Step 3 ◢ Draw an outline around the body. Add an eye, mouth, nostrils and claws.

Step 4 ◢ Add lots of little pencil lines for fur. Make the lines darker on the head, nose, and other face bits. Make darker lines for shadows too. Leave some places white or add a touch of white paint to make a shiny patch on its back.

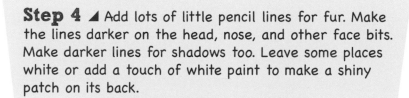

Look at me!

Guinea pigs aren't very smart, but they can be entertaining!

Two guinea pigs and a bit of lettuce

Scary sabre-toothed guinea pig!

Step 1 ▶ Draw big circles for their chests and rumps, with smaller circles for their heads.

Step 2 ▶ Add wedge shapes for noses and small circles for ears. Draw ovals for shoulders, lines for legs, and circles for knees. Sketch their feet.

Step 3 ◀ Draw outlines around their bodies, legs and feet. Don't forget their toes and claws!

Even a fit guinea pig isn't very thin!

Step 4 ◢ Colour them in. Make darker shades by going over the colour two or three times. Add fur and other details with pencil.

Rabbit

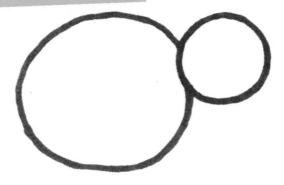

Step 1 ◢ Start with a big oval for his body and a smaller circle, just touching it, for the head.

Step 2 ▶ Add ovals for haunches, paws and a furry ruff under the head. Draw a small circle for a nose.

Step 3 ◀ Add a tail and long pointy ears. Draw an outline around the body and add a little eye.

Step 4 ▶ Draw lots of little pencil lines for fur and press harder for darker lines on the nose and ears. Leave a white spot on the eye, or add a touch of white paint to make it look bright.

Some rabbits are HUGE!

Wild rabbit

Step 1 ◀ Draw an oval for a middle, with two overlapping circles for the shoulders and rump.

Step 2 ◀ Add one oval for a head, another for a ruff, and a small circle for a nose. Draw lines for long legs and circles for knees, where the legs bend. Add ovals for big paws.

Step 3 ◣ Draw an outline around the body, adding two pointy ears and a tail. Add an oval for a cheek and a small eye above it.

Step 4 ▼ Colour with browns, greys and some orange. Leave some white underneath the body, and don't forget the whiskers!

A record-breaking bunny hop!

Lunch to go!

7

Hamster

Step 1 ◢ Start with a big circle for the shoulders, an overlapping circle for a body, and an overlapping oval for haunches.

Step 2 ◀ Add a circle for a head and an oval inside it for a face. Draw two small ears on top. Now the hamster is facing you!

Step 3 ▶ Draw two little circles for eyes and two circles below them for a muzzle. Sketch some toes.

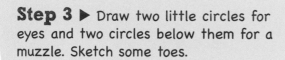

Hamsters can store food in their cheek pouches to eat later.

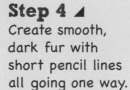

Greedy? Who, me?

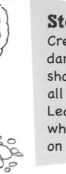

Step 4 ◢
Create smooth, dark fur with short pencil lines all going one way. Leave some bits white as markings on the fur.

Hamster on a wheel

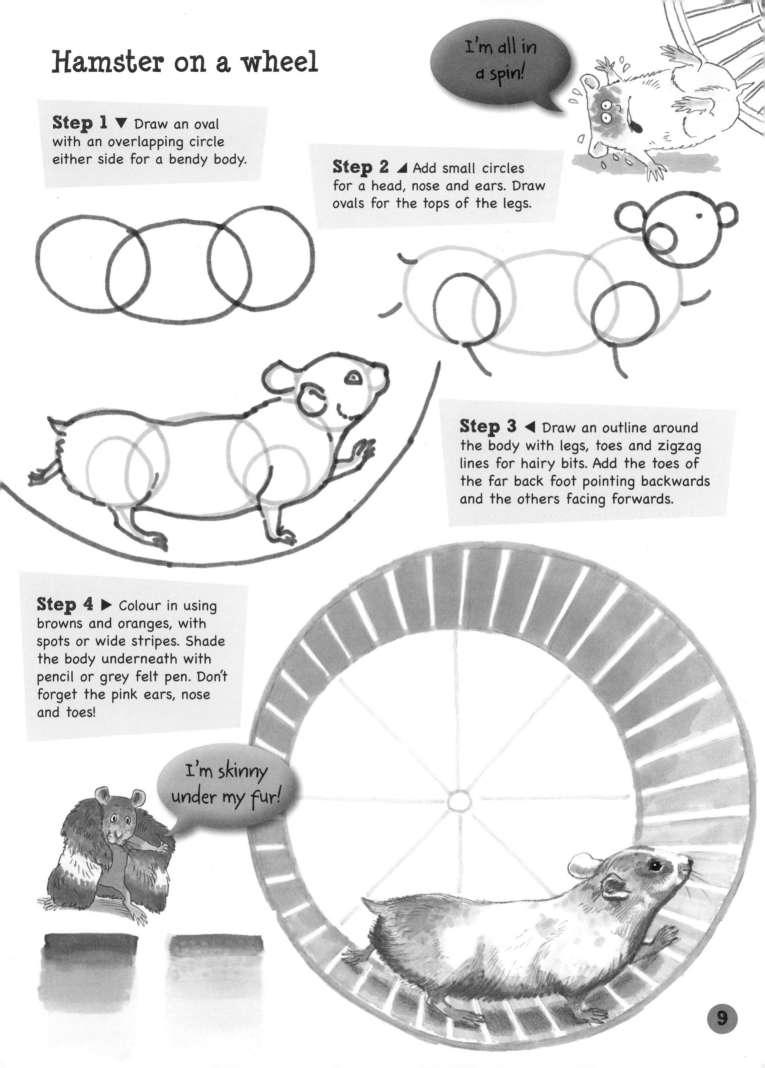

Step 1 ▼ Draw an oval with an overlapping circle either side for a bendy body.

Step 2 ◢ Add small circles for a head, nose and ears. Draw ovals for the tops of the legs.

I'm all in a spin!

Step 3 ◀ Draw an outline around the body with legs, toes and zigzag lines for hairy bits. Add the toes of the far back foot pointing backwards and the others facing forwards.

Step 4 ▶ Colour in using browns and oranges, with spots or wide stripes. Shade the body underneath with pencil or grey felt pen. Don't forget the pink ears, nose and toes!

I'm skinny under my fur!

Mouse

Step 1 ▼ Start with a big oval for the body and a circle inside for haunches. Add an overlapping circle for shoulders.

Step 2 ▼ Add a circle for a head, a smaller circle for a muzzle, and a tiny circle for a nose! Draw lines for legs and circles for knees.

Mice are easy to draw and mouse cartoons are fun!

Step 3 ▶ Draw an outline around the body, adding legs, ears and a long, curling tail. Add an eye and toes.

Step 4 ▼ Add lots of short pencil lines for fur, pressing harder for darker fur. Leave the tail and ears smooth.

Maybe it was all the blue cheese I ate!

Tee-hee!

Two pet mice

Step 1 ▶ Show these mice crouching rather than stretched out. First, draw two big circles for bodies, with small circles inside for shoulders and haunches. Leave room between the mice for their noses!

Step 2 ◀ Add small circles for heads with round ears on top. Add a little round nose and sketch in the legs and toes.

Huh?!

Step 3 ◀ Draw outlines around the bodies, legs and tails. One tail is curling behind and the other is curling in front.

Step 4 ◀ Colour your mice differently. The white mouse has pink eyes, but both have pink ears and tails!

Where's the cheese?

Cat

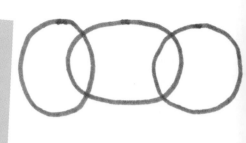

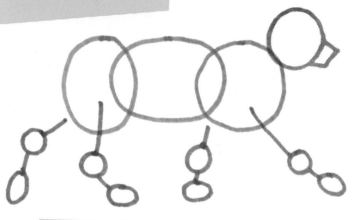

Step 1 ▶ Start by drawing a big oval for the middle, an overlapping circle for shoulders, and an overlapping circle for the rump.

Step 2 ▲ Add lines for legs with circles for knees and ovals for paws. Draw a circle for a head and a wedge for the muzzle. Notice that a walking cat has two paws on the floor at one time.

Step 3 ◀ Draw an outline around the body, legs and tail. Remember, the legs are furry and thick, and the tail long and fluffy. Add a triangle for one ear and a small tip for the other.

Step 4 ▶ Add a mouth, a triangular eye (although it is round when seen from the front), and a dainty nose. Have fun drawing the stripy fur!

Eeeek!

That's my line!

Leaping into the air!

Step 1 ▶ You'll show this cat's body stretched upwards, so draw the first shapes joined together but don't overlap them.

Step 2 ▶ Draw a circle for a head, a wedge for a muzzle, and a triangular ear. Draw circles and lines for knees and legs at full stretch.

Step 3 ◀ Draw an outline around the body, tail, legs and paws.

Step 4 ▲ Colour in with pale brown or cream. Add extra layers of colour to make darker stripes, especially over the back and tail.

Realistic colours and pretty patterns!

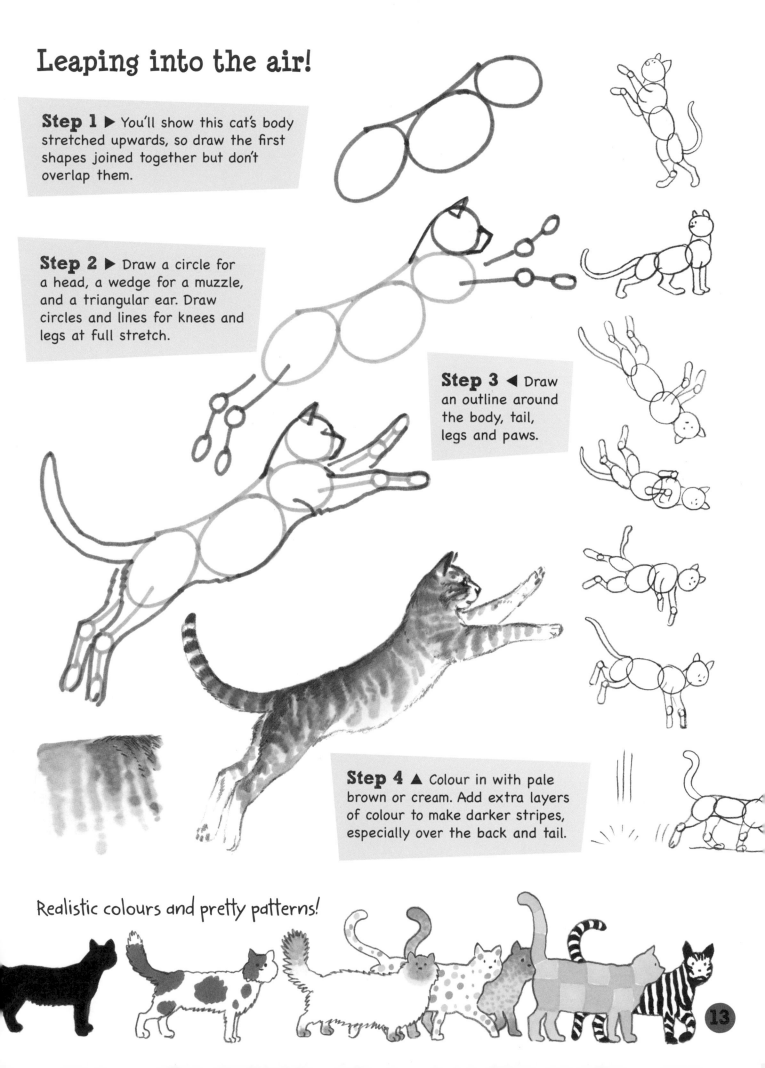

13

Gerbil

Step 1 ◀ To start, draw an oval for a body and an overlapping circle for a head.

Step 2 ▶ Add small circles on the face to help you draw the nose and mouth. Draw circles for shoulders and haunches, and little ears on the head.

Gerbils love to be with other gerbils!

Yummy!

Step 4 ▼ Draw long pencil lines for long hair and shorter lines for short hair. Use darker lines on the head. Leave a white spot on the eyes to make them look shiny.

Step 3 ◥ Draw an outline around the body, adding paws and a long, hairy tail. Draw little fingers, sharp claws and beady eyes.

Two friendly gerbils

Step 1 ▶ Draw round shapes for heads, shoulders and rumps. Put one gerbil slightly in front of the other one.

Gerbils like to take sand baths to keep their fur clean.

Nice tail, huh?

Step 2 ◣ Add circles for the ears and noses, as shown. Draw circles for shoulders and haunches.

Step 3 ◀ Draw outlines around the bodies, adding legs and tails. Draw eyes, claws and hairy tufts on the tails.

Step 4 ▶ Colour the gerbils' fur in pale or orangey brown. Add texture with pencil lines. Don't forget their black claws and pink noses!

What big teeth I have!

Dog

Yum!

Step 1 ▼ To start, draw an oval for a middle and an overlapping circle for shoulders. Add an oval for the rump and haunches, but set it at an angle as the dog will be standing with one leg back.

Step 2 ▼ Draw a circle for a head with a wedge for a muzzle. Add lines and circles for legs, knees and paws.

Step 3 ▼ Draw an outline around the body and legs, adding lots of little lines for a hairy underneath and tail. Draw a nose, eye, mouth, and paws. Add a big triangle for a floppy ear.

Step 4 ▼ Make the dog's coat look wavy. Draw a row of small lines curving one way, and another row of lines curving the other way.

Can't you see that I'm hiding?

Dog bounding!

Step 1 ▶ Start with the same three shapes as before but with the shoulders much higher than the back end. Can you see another oval at the back showing you what the far back leg is doing?

Step 2 ▶ Draw a circle for his head, overlapping the shoulders (your dog is facing you!). Add a half circle for a nose and two smaller circles underneath for a muzzle and chin. Draw lines where the ears and tail will go. Add lines and circles for the legs, knees and paws. Look at where the legs bend and cross over each other.

Step 3 ▶ Draw an outline around the body, legs and paws using lines and zigzags to show hair. Add eyes and a big smiling mouth.

Step 4 ▼ Colour in using brown, orange and yellow. Leave some light bits to show a paler coat and fur shining in the sun.

Happy! Happy! Happy!

Yelp! It's alive!

Stupid dog...

Good things come in small packages!

Shetland Pony

Step 1 ▼ Start with big circles overlapping an oval in the middle.

Step 2 ▼ Add a triangle for a neck and a wedge at the end for a head. Draw lines for legs and circles for knees and fetlocks (ankles). Add small lines at the end of the legs for hooves.

Step 3 ◄ Draw a half circle inside the head for a cheek and a circle at the end for a muzzle. Add an eye and a pointy ear. Draw an outline around the body and legs, with zigzag lines for a hairy mane and tail.

Oooh, nice!

Scratching an itchy bit.

Step 4 ▶ Draw lots of light pencil lines for shadows around the middle and rump. This shows the pony is round. Add lots of little pencil lines around the body outline for the hairy bits!

Bucking bronco!

Step 1 ◢ Draw an oval and two circles, as shown.

I can fly, too!

Step 2 ▶ Add a curved triangle for a neck and a wedge for a head. Add lines and circles for legs, knees and fetlocks. The front legs are on the ground and the back legs in the air.

Step 3 ▶ Draw an outline around the body and legs. Add triangles for hooves, a half circle for a cheek, and a circle for a muzzle. Draw a mouth, eye and ear. Add lines for a tail and mane.

Step 4 ◢ Colour in using creams and greys, but leave lots of white. Draw pencil lines for hair on the mane, tail and fetlocks. Add shadows in pencil on the stomach and far legs to make your pony look real.

Ponies come in lots of colours - let your imagination run wild!

19

Details

Shading

Try out different pencils. The ones marked HB or B have harder lead and make lighter lines. Pencils marked 2B or 4B have softer lead and make darker lines.

Make a 2D (two-dimensional) circle into a 3D (three-dimensional) ball using shading.

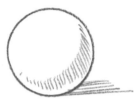

▲ Little light straight lines.

▲ Cross-hatching with a softer pencil.

▲ Shading with the side of the pencil.

Textures

▼ Different lines for hair and fur.

▶ Use the basic shapes you start each drawing with to help you put shading in the right place.

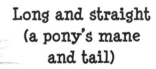

Straight and short (mouse fur)

Long and straight (a pony's mane and tail)

Short and curvy (gerbil fur)

Long and wavy (dog hair)

Noses and Tails

Noses and tails are important. Can you tell which ones belong to which pet?

How silly would it look if they got mixed up!

Backgrounds

Grass is easy to do...
Use different shades of green markers to make grass look interesting and create a sense of depth. Draw lighter green first and darker green over the top.

Play games with scale!
Draw a giant hamster or a tiny pony in a grass forest! You could write a story to go with it.

What do they sit on? Where do they sleep?

Study your own pets and think about how to draw them.

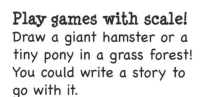

Do they like to use the furniture or make nests?

It's fun to think about where your pets come from. Wild gerbils live in dry deserts and they like burrowing.

Where does your pet live?

Has it ever escaped?

Straw helps pets keep warm, and it's easy to draw with just a few random pencil lines. Use light and dark yellows and add pencil lines over the top.

Practise your drawing...

Start SIMPLE
Practise your shapes – ovals, circles, squares, wedges and triangles.

Use good quality pencils and double-ended felt pens. These have useful thick and thin ends which are really great for colouring and blending.

Now let's put them together to create some great animal drawings!

Remember to use texture
and shading to make your
animals look realistic!